# Jeremiad Johnson

# Dedication

To Jane, who instilled in me a love of books, and to Tim, who is the biggest booster and promoter of the ones I write.

And to Gibby, Sam and Dave, who fill me with pride and my days with joy.

**In Case Of Emergency Press**

*http://www.icoe.com.au*

# Jeremiad Johnson

*Tim Hawkins*

# Acknowledgements

The author gratefully acknowledges the publications in which many of the poems collected in Jeremiad Johnson first appeared:

**13 Miles from Cleveland**: "Task Force," "When the Pages All Fall Out"
**The Big Windows Review**: "Improvisation in Autumn"
**Blue Lake Review**: "An Offering"
**Iron Horse Literary Review**: "Birth of the Three-Headed Calf"
**KYSO Flash**: "A Long Broken Passage," "Two Brothers"
**The Literary Bohemian**: "Freight," "Siesta"
**Sixfold**: "Animal Planet," "The Archives," "Burn and Linger," "The Eclipse," "The Gallery," "Just Now," "The Leap," "Northern Idyll"
**The Smoking Poet**: "Stones"
**Tipton Poetry Journal**: "A Brush with Royalty," "Gaius Cassius Longinus Breaks the Fourth Wall", "The Death of a Colleague"
**Underground Voices Magazine**: "The Old Fighting Spirit," "On Why the Problem Goes Well Beyond Drinking"
**Valparaiso Poetry Review**: "Southern Gothic"
**Verse Wisconsin**: "Tonight's Broadcast"

"Tonight's Broadcast" also appeared in the collection, **Wanderings at Deadline** (Aldrich Press, 2012)

# Foreword

Film fans and those of my generation are probably familiar with the 1972 Sydney Pollack film, *Jeremiah Johnson*, starring Robert Redford as a mid-19th century trapper and hunter trying to survive in the harsh landscape of the mountainous North American West—a character based on an historical and semi-legendary figure with the imposing name of John "Liver-Eating" Johnson. It is one of the "old movies" my children didn't want to watch, but quickly became a family favourite.

The historical "Liver-Eating" Johnson was known for eating the organs of his sworn enemies, the Crow, a habit the film chooses not to depict. Our 21st century Johnson is not known to be a consumer of enemy livers, but he is nonetheless filled with bile. Sporting a common surname, derived from every European language with a John, Jan, Jens, Johan or Johannes, this "son of John" is a very common kind of man trying to survive and make do in our contemporary society a century and a half after Jeremiah Johnson and more than two millennia after the original Jeremiah, "the weeping prophet," of the Old Testament, who prophesied Jerusalem's destruction and from whose name the term "jeremiad" derives.

These poems are Johnson's bilious jeremiad, his prolonged lamentation, complaint, screed, rant, cautionary tale and harangue—by turns irascible, peevish, chastened and accepting. While "Liver-Eating" Johnson somehow survived into his seventies, the fictional Jeremiah Johnson, after making peace with the Crow, likely met his lonely demise fording a river in midwinter or in the crush of an avalanche. This century's Johnson may suffer a heart attack in the company breakroom a week before his retirement or keel over shovelling snow from the end of his driveway. Hopefully his jeremiad will linger for a season or two.

**Tim Hawkins**

Published by In Case of Emergency Press 2019

Copyright © Tim Hawkins 2019

All rights reserved. Without limiting the rights under copyright reserved above, no part of this publication may be reproduced, stored in or introduced into a database and retrieval system or transmitted in any form or any means (electronic, mechanical, photocopying, recording or otherwise) without the prior written permission of both the owner of copyright and the above publishers.

ISBN 978-0-9943525-3-8

Jeremiad Johnson

# Table of contents

| | |
|---|---|
| TONIGHT'S BROADCAST | 1 |
| TASK FORCE | 3 |
| THE DEATH OF A COLLEAGUE | 4 |
| GAIUS CASSIUS LONGINUS BREAKS THE FOURTH WALL | 6 |
| JUST NOW | 7 |
| BURN AND LINGER | 8 |
| THE LEAP | 9 |
| NORTHERN IDYLL | 10 |
| TWO BROTHERS | 11 |
| SOUTHERN GOTHIC | 12 |
| FREIGHT | 14 |
| A BRUSH WITH ROYALTY | 16 |
| THE ECLIPSE | 17 |
| NOTES ON A MISSPENT YOUTH | 18 |
| THE OLD FIGHTING SPIRIT | 20 |
| ON WHY I FAILED THEM | 22 |
| AN OFFERING | 24 |
| IMPROVISATION IN AUTUMN | 25 |
| THE GALLERY | 26 |
| ANIMAL PLANET | 27 |
| SIESTA | 28 |
| A LONG BROKEN PASSAGE | 29 |
| SOLILOQUY | 30 |
| ON WHY THE PROBLEM GOES WELL BEYOND DRINKING | 31 |
| STONES | 32 |
| BIRTH OF THE THREE-HEADED CALF | 34 |
| WHEN THE PAGES ALL FALL OUT | 35 |
| THE ARCHIVES | 36 |
| ABOUT THE AUTHOR | 39 |

*Jeremiad Johnson*

*Jeremiad Johnson*

*There are smells in this book, but only in this book and not in the world. There is freshly cut grass, but only in this book and not in the world. There is someone speaking to me, someone I can understand, but only in this book. When I close the cover and look out, the world is a gabble of foreign tongues that love themselves all over and clamour for more love.*

from 'When the Pages All Fall Out'

*Jeremiad Johnson*

*Tim Hawkins* *Jeremiad Johnson*

## Tonight's Broadcast

Tonight's broadcast is all but drowned out
by my fellow small-town diners, who, with the ring
of a bell take refuge from the late autumn chill.

But I gather from the flickering TV that pedestrians
still stalk the impatient sidewalks of our great cities
resigned to life's thousands of petty grievances.

I can feel their fatigue in my bones,
the ankle twisted on the subway stairs,
and the need for a drink;

even, while at the same time,
a group of boys in another part of the city
divines the future in a heap of broken glass.

Here in the hinterlands, Dolores, the waitress
in her faded grey dress, refills my coffee
and with quivering lips conveys her pride
that her boy has gone off to serve.

From throughout this patch of the provinces
and all across the land, boys in their prime
are cut down like winter wheat.

I start to tell her something, but she turns
and doesn't hear; one more voice, like the clatter
of cutlery, added to the general din.

Most of the folks in here are also tired,
and try to keep warm from the steam of their coffee
that rises to shroud the windows.

But the banker with the bright pink face
and the doughy hands seems jolly; he cracks
a joke and winks as Dolores walks away.

*Jeremiad Johnson*                                                                                 *Tim Hawkins*

I'm not sure why I want to take a meat cleaver to his fat fingers,
since I am as complicit in all of this as he,
and he did, after all, once almost approve me for a loan.

But, before I leave, I lean across his booth to write
a few choice words in the steam of the window, then
once out the door, kick a frozen doughnut to the curb.

# Task Force

I am taken aback that so many seem
to become so energized by this process
of producing a plan to produce a plan
that has less and less to do with trees and concrete and
more and more to do with a fractured agenda
and the sound of words strung together
by the force of the human voice, so unlike
the sound of poetry or even prose.
I would suggest that some are still running
for class president of the seventh grade
if I wasn't so busy hanging out
by the water fountain looking cool,
and scribbling these marginal notes.
I will concede that there is plenty of direction
in this document, and there are more
than a few data. However, given
the absence of consensus, I would motion
that we adjourn from this sound-proof room
out into the bright afternoon, to get ourselves
back on track, to commit some tasks, with force,
the way a child might envision our mandate.
We might also just clasp hands in silence
in a huddled mass on the carpeted floor
to escape this maelstrom of discourse
devoid of perspective, context and common sense,
to remember the way things were before we came in here,
and the way things are outside so many rooms.
Or, barring these unlikely eventualities,
might I suggest, that we make certain, at the very least
to peruse the support materials, these
lovely, leather-clad briefing books
that someone has so kindly assembled for our edification,
before next week's penultimate session?

## The Death of a Colleague

Because it happened in real time,
right there in the break room
at the base of the moulded plastic bench
not far from the non-dairy creamers
within sight of the microwave,
those of us who witnessed it
could barely recognize it for what it was.

At first it was inextricable from the banal.
I remember a cell phone ringing
and someone dropping a spoon,
and the violent clacking of heels
echoing down the corridor.
Then there was a whisper,
which brought us up short and in close,
and a concentration of fluorescent light
shining off his forehead,
some spittle and a gagging sound.

Of course someone made a call,
and someone loosened the poor man's tie
and someone said "Oh, my dear God,"
and someone asked "Does anyone know CPR?"
and someone screamed (sorry,
the company insists on anonymity).

But quickly, all of us there came to know
a sudden and unspeakable finality,
the kind still found in what we like
to call the natural world–
a re-alighting of the vulture
after a young animal has fallen.

I recall that we left as a group, escorted
out by a handsome young man from HR,
bearing away a handful of small
and inconsequential possessions,
including the iPhone 8, whose screen
showed a smiling wife and daughter.

Well, things soon got back to normal
and the office returned to its smooth
daily rhythms ("Thank, God!"),
and after an intensive round of grief
counselling, there were smiles all around
and the inevitable sense of closure.

## Gaius Cassius Longinus Breaks the Fourth Wall

*—After Shakespeare's Julius Caesar (I, ii)*

Another lapse in reason at the top
Displaying yet more hubris than the last.
We've grown exhausted asking to what depths
This Caesar may sink before he's called to task
To answer for his rancid petulance.
The Grand Old Party leaders have decamped
From bully pulpits where they might stand tall
Like Antony, who with one heartfelt speech
Turned all of Rome against our noble band.
*So are they all, all honourable men...*

The boss, meanwhile, sounds out his entourage
Whose murmurings plumb the depths of his just cause.
Not for the first time wonder strikes me dumb
As I consider just how much is lost.
*Why, man, he doth bestride the narrow world*
Where he, alone, is master of our fates.
Yet, needlessly, he circumscribes that orb
To circumnavigate with baby steps.

*Now, in the names of all the gods at once,*
*Upon what meat do these our Caesars feed,*
*That they are grown so great? Age, thou art shamed...*
By harlequins who play the role of kings.
Tell me again what brought us to this place
Where narrow interests forge a brittle peace
That propagates unnatural human states
By prying man from gods and young from old?
Where families fly apart like airborne seeds
And in the windswept darkness take up root.

On this, like so much else, the pundits clash
With wars of words torn from the holy books,
While alienated men retreat to caves
To write God's name in smoke across the skies.
Great Caesar has no answer, just more Tweets,
Yet Caesar wields a rudimentary tool:
The wedge that drives our citizens apart.

## Just Now

Just now, after a day spent
retouching scarred decades
of scuff marks on a hardwood floor,

after a day spent repairing generations
of gouges inflicted on sturdy joists and beams
once hoisted on strong, nineteenth-century backs,

admiring, all the while, the legacy
of sound masonry and stately moulding
wrought by precise and careful handiwork;

just now, taking a break
on a late afternoon in early summer,

I look out through the plate glass
of this centuries-old storefront
and witness the rarest and finest of showers:

a sun-dappled burst from nowhere
against a backdrop of robin-egg
blue and rose-coloured sky.

Every age perfects its own handiwork
and leaves a masterpiece of flint, obsidian, stone
bronze, iron, marble
plutonium or silicon.

Nevertheless,
so much sudden, wanton, cruel
maddening beauty abounds,
that each generation runs out of time
before it can really even
begin to describe

a sun-dappled burst from nowhere
or the first blush of a maiden's cheek.

## Burn and Linger

I won't want any of this to be about me, per se.
In the beginning I'll want to just disappear
into another continent, into another culture,
to submerge myself into centuries of tradition
like fleets of ancestral fishermen crossing a treacherous reef.

But after a while, I suppose I'll also want to burn,
at least a little.

I'll want to smoulder
like paper money stoked for the comfort of my ancestors,
like a waking god hoisted on the shoulders of my acolytes,
and to flow through the scene
like the smoke of joss sticks drifting from a temple,
like a flaming boat built solely for the burning.

And of course, after all is said and done,
I'll want to linger.

I'll want to remain like the scent of lemongrass
after you have walked a moonlit trail,
the shy water buffalo calf trailing after,
but not like the bone clattering of bamboo
announcing its exaggerated growth.

I'll long to awaken
on the temple steps at dawn,
with something plucked and desired
in hand.

A plum, perhaps
—delicious, dark and cool to the touch—
or something else that burns
and lingers through a ripe
and darkening age.

# The Leap
### —for David

I hold your small hand in mine
while salmon lunge
and hurt themselves
on the rocks beneath us,
chasing death,
immortality
and a dim and watery notion
of home.

In the not-too-distant past,
folks from the east side of town
arrived in horse carts and carriages
on this bluff above the river,
hailing one another
in the cool of evening
as they gaped at the bounding rapids
and the bears
who fished below.

With a promise of ice cream in hand,
we make our way to the car
parked on the bluff—
now a park
surrounded by hospitals,
apartments
and schools.

One day you will return without me
and you will understand
like the generations of salmon and men,
that though the bears and horse carts
may be gone,
the poorly understood migrations
and countless wet dreams
remain.

## Northern Idyll

Flushed and fevered, appalled by the city,
you crept through nightfall over shards of glass
back to the northern forest, whence you'd come;

An upland preserve of bear wallow and fattening deer
where tannic alder and maple-soaked rivers cool
like a tonic the colour of tea or bourbon,
depending on your need.

You had planned to wade their timeless eddies,
to meander in their cloudy back currents,
to imagine lost loves and idylls
and absent friends,

until the night I arrived at your door
with furrowed brow and frown as tight
as my clenched and trembling fist
to solve the latter once and for all,

and to bring word from the late city
with its campaign slogans and broken bottles,
scorched pavement and red-rimmed,
downcast eyes,

word of the woman and child denied
this leafy province of despair.

## Two Brothers

*—for Chey*

The west wind blows his rail thin silhouette
slouching back to town as Halloween
fades, scattering my middle class pieties
like discarded wrappers at the children's feet.

He gnaws on domesticity like a bone,
leaving gristle on my lumpy sofa bed,
humouring my good intentions like a faithful dog
who would eat his way through you for his freedom.

At some point, as frost gathers on the horizon,
I begin to mutter about values and hard choices,
though, occasionally, I too, long to sleep in contentment
beneath the piano, or to wake with leaves in my hair.

Then, just like that, without a word he sets off again, the children
with fewer tears and questions as they grow accustomed,
and I, with no reliable information
about where he sleeps tonight.

Many possibilities—alleys and boxcars
or wrapped in plastic out beneath the pines—
though I try hard not to imagine.

Instead, I settle for tossing and turning,
playing the piano, and contemplating
sleeping in late from time to time.

## Southern Gothic

Artefacts strewn and scattered among the ruins,
heaped alongside the teetering barn,
propped against fence posts with falling-down rails–
an iron rooster weather vane
divines the turmoil at our feet,
a rusted pump handle points the way
to a wood stove and spring house
set in dry creek beds run to mockery.

What are these things, the children ask?
And I hardly know how to answer,
for whatever I propose for this *mise-en-scène*
will never do it justice.

The one is for cooking biscuits, I say,
the other a cool place for black snakes
and spiders in the heat of day,
both anachronistic as the hand grinder,
the cotton gin, the Underwood typewriter,
the sweet smell of boxwoods and clover,
the loveliness of fresh mown hay...

But they've already lost interest
as other guests begin to arrive–
a rag man come to stitch a handmade doll;
a sharpener of knives all set to carve
a sheaf of silhouettes;
an unseen fox, perhaps, from up in the hills,
to scatter the plump due diligence of hens
while flightless turkeys roost on the splintered rails.

Luminous evening of honeysuckle and cornbread,
wisteria and magnolia blossom, please
bring forth the coolness of absolution, we pray.
For grasshoppers whir in barren fields
as hot and acrid as spit tobacco,
toads and all manner of creatures
are stymied and shrivel in the heat,
and dust rises for miles along the washboard road.

## Freight

I tried for years to write of trains,
to catch the rhythm of their churning wheels
in the uneven flow of words,

to put one word past another
like endless tracks stealing across
three vast and stubborn continents,

to remember your hand in mine
across the eternal moonscape
distance of the western states, and watch
your true face appear by morning light,

to yearn to be with you, apart
from the wayward Midwestern looks,
in some private rolling space
where longing is no destination.

I tried for years to find the words
to comfort the sobbing German girl
whose stolen bag is politely returned
while the polite train waits, and the
culprit is shot on the bloodstained tracks
in the remoter wastes of Xinjiang.

I tried for years to stop the wailing
of beggars as we slow to take on fuel,
then speed up again through a nightmare
haze of midnight villages,

to bring to life the dying child
thrust half-through an open window
by her screaming mother stumbling along
the uneven tracks of Varanasi.

## Jeremiad Johnson

For many years now, a good long while,
I have ridden the lines of commuter rail,
where I read the front page twice a day
and the headlines of Sports and Metro.

But the trains roll by, all night long
to the infinite freight yards of Chicago,
and shake my house to the basement walls
as I toss and turn in my sleep.

*Jeremiad Johnson*  *Tim Hawkins*

# A Brush with Royalty

Somehow, by the time I bothered to look up
it was almost spring again
and most of us had survived the winter,
though last year it had seemed there were pines as far as the eye could see,
and I remembered something about a chickadee.

But then I caught the pear tree at full glance.
And at once, as if shrugging off the season's hold,
as if looking back centuries, it was autumn's final day again
or winter's first, and I found as I fondled the tree's final offering
of the season, that inside the split, frost-puckered skin of that pear,
its pulpy flesh was gaudily alive with shimmering sequins
blazing with warmth and light.

In the way they kept their own counsel and disdained my proffered hand,
I felt I had discovered something akin to beleaguered aristocrats
and their last vestige of a more regal way of life:
a full retinue of ladybugs squired by a final squadron of wasps
each keeping to its own distinct lobe, yet preparing, nonetheless,
to winter together in that hovel of shrivelled fruit.

At the core of this most succulent of fruits grown overripe,
I had the fleeting notion of abdicating royalty in flight
and the sensation of finding something precious
like a Faberge egg mislaid among all of the looting;

And of peering into it against a backdrop of grey and desolate boulevards
leading out past a parade ground of wind-chapped and ill-fed recruits
going through the motions of a drill,

a grim and silent rehearsal
for totalitarian winter's
seemingly offhand regicide.

## The Eclipse

The early evening light leaves the room discreetly
as if a second skin is expected to arrive,
and a periodic rustling of air
slips through the beige curtain
to pass over the prone, naked body
like the inspired breath of lips.

When darkness finally settles in,
the ice in a glass has melted
and the liquid is warm as blood
where a ring has formed
on the dark, solid wood of the night table,
on which grows a faint scent like ferns
in the loam of the forest floor.

For a boundless, solitary moment, the body,
at perfect equipoise, without hunger or desire,
grows womblike within the desolate confines
of its hairless planes and slackening breath.

But before the darkness can even pass
there begin the first, faint, telltale stirrings
of the spirit, a desire to anthropomorphize
the motives of light and air
and a need to outlast and exhaust
the perfect moment,

a self-awareness provoked
perhaps, by the proximity
of blood and ferns,
a primal awakening inspired
and informed by
terror.

# Notes on a Misspent Youth

By way of late night rambles and incursions
on self-styled missions from God,
staggering under starlight
through profound and absurdist landscapes
toward the gleam of an illicit dawn,
always in search of some
mosaic of unfathomable light:

In the focused glare of the congregation's wrath
at the dishevelled stranger in its midst,
in the swirling sparks of a late Spring snowstorm
as seen upon waking with leaves in his hair,
in the sheen of saffron robes and curses of the monk
who kicks the sleeping figure from the steps of his temple,
in the laughter of certain people
perhaps touched by grace—or at least by charm,
in the soft pre-dawn stirring of the woodlands
and in the soft summer rain, always in the rain.

Once, for just a moment, after hours of contemplation,
through late afternoon into the gathering cold of nightfall
in the silence of wintering pines, he thought he heard
the voice of God begin to speak,
but was interrupted by a chipmunk's alarum.

\* \* \*

Up today at first light
to balance his chequebook and water the lawn.
Things and events and people do not swim together;
there remains, nowadays, a solid, satisfying separation.
The houses of the neighbours, even in this first, faint haze,
like developing Polaroids
gradually regain their solidity
and their impressive mass and size.

Tim Hawkins

Jeremiad Johnson

Only some longhaired kid in a rumpled sweatshirt
to disrupt the scene and cause this flood of recollections,
an unknown neighbour boy stumbling home through the suburbs
through the first pink glow of dawn
with love and God and bliss and hair
in his eyes, gliding homeward
toward obsolescence.

*Jeremiad Johnson*                                                          *Tim Hawkins*

# The Old Fighting Spirit

I remember the fight,
one of many—
me and John Coletti in the backyard
and his brother Marco standing by
should things get out of hand,

and the old man, who happened to let the dog out
if I'm getting the worst of it,
which in this case I am—

and my odd reaction,
calling a time out,
being let up to put the dog in the garage,
then resuming my position
on the bottom.

Was this the passionless spirit of "fair play"
that made the country great?

Ask the Lakota, the bison, the woodchuck,
the two-legged and the four,
anything and everything that stood in the way.

With what courteous fate had I been negotiating?

And then, years later,
standing there watching her go,
performing with perfect equanimity:

"It is, after all, her life, her right, her decision.
What good would it do to smash the windows
and beg her to stay?"

Sometime later I finally understood the futility of my efforts,
and broke off all negotiations with a calm, dispassionate fate:

"Life has kept its promises, boy. Who ever asked you to accept them?

Scream and beg and plead and maim.
Kill yourself, then her,
then everyone else in the vicinity.
Kill them all
to make sure you get
the right one.

Now you've got it."

*Jeremiad Johnson*                                                              *Tim Hawkins*

# On Why I Failed Them

For whoever is keeping track
about this Romeo here
and his Juliet, both so eager
to leap right out of the page,

whom I had wanted so badly,
among all the others,
to take my platitudes to heart,

who were so young they never knew
that I, like every adult in their lives,
had helped to doom them from the start,

a word of explanation about them and all the rest
in the space reserved for comments
next to that of the final test:

Like the Nurse I clucked, an eager hen
so full of seeming mischief,
so quick with a joke while my soul sat in brood
on the egg of conventional wisdom.

Like good Friar Laurence I pled and scolded, and feared
for my students' (intellectual) damnation.
As my schemes fell apart, I fled from the tomb
and scampered for home,
in fear of the Prince's watchmen.

But come morning I slouched, fully contrite,
back to the boneyard
where ideas go to die in the hot, white glare,
where, by its charter, there is not much left
to wonder, imagine or dare.

And duly reinstated, we pondered the trite
and made a great show of our answers being right,
then sat idly by and chewed our tongues
as if we awaited news from Friar John,
who set off for hope and Mantua
and stepped into a house of plague.

But he never returned,
and so we sat and no one spoke
while we waited for something more,
but they never even bore
the bodies in procession
back to the stage.

And the Prince never bothered to make his speech,
nor Montague his pledge
(We found out later, second-hand,
they were unavoidably detained).

And so we sat, as if on edge,
our sun-burnt eyes blinked into the sun,
and finally the bell and we made to speak,
but our mouths had filled with sand;

and no one trembled with rage.

# An Offering

Do you remember the hour
you tumbled naked, headlong
out of sleep and the burning sky?

You found yourself, frail and stumbling
in a landscape of bone and tumbling waters,
picking berries alone,

wandering from thicket to thicket
as the juice ran in crimson tears
from the corners of your smile.

This is all I need of you:
an offering of words, like berries
collected in the loneliest hour of that day.

Whisper some small true words
not spit from the mouths
of friends,
not coughed out gasping
from another life.

Whisper some small true words
bearing the scars of your teeth and
we shall savour the harvest with our tongues.

Offer your gathering of summer storms,
or the branches trembling in your winter sky.
Offer the night moving in you.

Make an offering
of the silences roaring within
and we shall have no more need of words.

We will share
armloads or mouthfuls
of any berry you like,

first gathered in days of rage,
ripened and burning like skin,
then cooled in night-blooming silence.

## Improvisation in Autumn

I'm mindful of those who feel some peril in the change of season
bringing an end to the confusion
of night-blooming flowers and open windows
—a sudden, calamitous chill of clarity
in the precipitous drop
from late summer to sudden fall.

And I'm mindful of those who realize that surviving
the dead calm menace of our dog days
and close afternoons of buzzing flies
is no guarantee of spring.

To some children, I suppose, summer is already a half-remembered fiesta
whose rain-soaked confetti lies unnoticed along the roadside,
while for others there may remain troubling dreams
of twilight deer and fireflies.

I could mention a host of others:
the stranger whose arms grow thinner with each passing year,
the bruised young wife who sobs into her fists—not for the final time,
and those who look away from the others and from themselves
when their lives pass in the street.

As a courtesy I might also mention
the rain and the swaying branches
that form the backdrop to the pageant of their lives.

Or I could just stop and admit
to an awkward sort of contrived spontaneity
in this poem, which in some sense, at least,
mirrors much about those lives:

a failed improvisation on the whole, but a performance, nonetheless,
containing seeds of promise and moments of light,
not to mention the usual passel of lies
and a cast of thousands.

## The Gallery

My wife was born in a tropical climate
where trees flourish through sun and rain
and the four seasons are a myth passed down
and diluted like generations of conquistador blood.

Here, in Michigan, she is fascinated by the falling leaves,
how some nights they swirl and dance across the road
seeming to perform for our oncoming headlights,
and she chides me for failing to notice such beauty.

Thanks to her insistence I now have another experience
to reconsider, another image to call to mind
in the cold and austere days that will come
soon enough, in the long, white gallery of winter.

# Animal Planet

While we bow our heads to the ground
and our hearts seek meaning among the stars,
wild creatures assert their presence
in the here and now
and the just here and gone.

Unknowable in the way one speaks
of the alien and other-worldly,
the title to their kingdom is forged
in their absolute
manifestation of the flesh.

If this seems ironic and abstract,
then so be it.

For irony and abstraction
are our great gifts—
not to the world, but to ourselves—
invented for our survival.

And we, of course, are the real aliens;
Each a world unto one's own,
orbiting a sun of its own devising.

## Siesta

These latitudes bring unaccustomed blessings
like mangoes falling on my tin-roofed shack,
the solitude to hear my own confession,
and penance that renounces all I lack.

I've passed a grateful season on this couch
in rooms as stark and naked as a prayer
with plywood walls in need of human touch
and fingers tracing nothing in the air.

But outside in the garden where the rains
entreat a teeming lushness from the earth
lianas, epiphytes, and creeping vines
enact a strangling forest of rebirth.

At rest, I lie untouched above the fray
with fragrant strife and rumours of decay.

## A Long Broken Passage

On horseback, at night, winding slowly skyward
through dry-season wash, amid outcropping boulders,
past sluggish, latent rattlesnake, hibernacula of lizard,
stars so near at hand, so crystalline,
so close to the mountain I can reach up
and cut my wrists on their jagged contours.

I feel the warmth of the horse pass through me;
our steady exhalations rise as one.

Not far off a wildcat screams,
flushing a covey of night-roosting doves.
A whirlwind, the clatter of hooves on stone,
and yet my horse remains composed.
Steadfast, she gathers herself beneath me.

Sitting alone, above it all, rocking toward the heavens,
my cold, shaking hand strokes the side of her neck
as if reaching into a rushing current.
I imagine that over the next dark ridge
we will come to a sudden halt,
face-to-face with a bold white horse
in the sagebrush-scented moonlight.

It is a long broken passage back down
to the land of all things familiar, back down
to the smell of oats and dust and manure.

The game birds, the reptiles, the horse and I,
the stars—we all must die. We know this.
But since I know so little of wildcats
or white horses for that matter,
and dust does not rely on timely arrivals,
we may tarry for just a while longer
among the sagebrush and boulders.

## Soliloquy

I mounted the stage of my youth
with such suppleness and strength,
and with such anticipation to know,
imagine, and feel greatness.

After a while I grew into my role,
no longer hamming it up for cheap applause;
I got to the point where I could play my part
with my mind on other matters.

But, in a kind of dramatic irony,
I happen to know something that the audience
does not: the more I appeared to move them,
the less I was able to actually feel.

The longer I trod the boards, the more desperate
I became, impotent and out of breath,
diminished in my capacity to feel anything
besides anxiety to hit my mark.

Apart from one stabbing look of betrayal
that brought down the house,
the details became interchangeable,
the audience laughter predictable,
the scene changes awkward,
the dialogue stilted,
the plot stale.

I plead my case now to a darkened house,
asking no one in particular:

"Why do we bother to collect these experiences at all?
To fill an empty box with more emptiness
and fasten it all with a ribbon of irony?"

The curtain descends on a Sunday matinee
and the air fills with dust.

Feral dogs roam the city,
the doors are thrust open,
and a warm wind blows boldly through the house.

## On Why the Problem Goes Well Beyond Drinking

No impure substances for fifteen months;
my head now feels about as big as the world
and my heart is just as small.

Imagine you'd always dreamed of a place,
had come to find that it didn't really exist,
but were okay as long as you didn't admit that to yourself.
Now you don't even bother looking for that place anymore.

The old mansion has no more mysterious rooms to explore.
You've been relegated to a shotgun shack, where every room
is within footsteps and you know every square inch of the house
because you pace it and pace it, though your footsteps make no sound.

Give me another kind of cell: an empty bar somewhere near the water,
an ocean breeze, clack of bamboo, twinkle of lights, and clamour of
wind chimes.
Give me a place to drink silently and with a purpose, circling, spiralling
spastically down, down into the deep blue like the dead or dying shark.

## Stones

Mined from quarries, plucked from meadows,
gathered near lakesides throughout the ages
by gnarled and practiced, earth-whorled thumbs,
we may know them as "Oldowan bifaces

giving rise to the Acheulean handaxe," or simply as
"rocks," but by any name they left their mark–
cutting, hacking, scraping, and cleaving their way onto
the fossilized bones that remain and the many that do not.

As skill became tradition, and ultimately industry,
generations learned from their elders the skills of knapping
fragile knife points, skipping flat ones across placid streams,
and punishing with blunt force the joys of a young adulteress.

\*\*\*

On your way out the door, as the grey
thunderhead gathered for the first slap of rain,
you thought of stones
and their blunt, worn-away contours–

tumbling, moss-covered stones loosened
from moorings with the early inundations of spring,
heavy boulders rolled away from empty tombs,
pebbles resting upon the eyes of the dead.

Just before the first thunderclap spread
a sheet of icy symmetry across
the broad and deepening river,
and you failed to see the trees and their changing leaves,

you thought of stones—
their solid but empty thud against flesh
and their sharp, splintering
crack against bone,

as you pocketed them one after another
in this time of war, weighing your certainty
with numb but practiced fingers
a few short steps from the slippery bank.

## Birth of the Three-Headed Calf

In the blood-spent aftermath, the oxen clatter ceases and
the wagon wheels groan to a halt as the child in black
arrives to bring word to the last of the outlying settlements,
and the wind shudders through the marshes.

*Tim Hawkins*                                                        *Jeremiad Johnson*

# When the Pages All Fall Out

Things flatten out to two dimensions.
There are no longer smells in the world.
Easily overlooked, I become my surroundings,
easing into the cool and soothing corner
away from the sun-blasted corridors.
No one calls to me in gibberish here
and the favourite books lie nearby,
prized possessions, inscribed by friends,
that I have lugged all over the world
in these strangely diminished hands,
that now teem with new inscriptions
of spider web, insect larvae, and
sentences I am unable to decipher,
as yet another page flutters out.
When the pages all fall out
I will have read the book.

There are smells in this book, but only in this book
and not in the world. There is freshly cut grass,
but only in this book and not in the world. There is
someone speaking to me, someone I can understand,
but only in this book. When I close the cover and
look out, the world is a gabble of foreign tongues
that love themselves all over and clamour for
more love.

## The Archives

After the stabbing light of the sun
has dimmed to a wintery ache in the eye,
one grows accustomed to stark interiors,
intimate with corridors
and their convolutions
of gun-metal grey.

After a certain period of adjustment
amid the superficial scrape and glint
of marble halls and their distorted
echoes of coughing like laughter
in the rarefied air,

after the clatter of metal slamming
and footsteps marching away in lockstep,
then fading along the corridor,

something rare that we are gifted
and burdened to name
is bred in the silence that follows
and filed away.

There is a veneer of winter solitude
that can linger then, briefly,
like snowfall melting on clothing

or that can remain for a longer term
like wintering in some forest hollow,
marking a more remote frontier,
a knife's claim on ragged bone
bounded by a feverish wind.

Perhaps that is the end of it, after all,
a sudden shiver, an abrupt decision
followed by the tinkling of ice
and a return to the sunny port
of conviviality.

Or perhaps, after numerous seasons,
after window-less years spent
locked in dutiful chambers
by turns airless or draughty,
idly tracing the torn and faded map
of one's veins,

from some half-remembered story
rescued from the false bottom
of memory
one hears apocryphal footsteps
creeping away
along the chilly corridor
among the snowy drifts—

a second self
cloaked in the terrible
gift or burden
of a second skin.

One imagines archival landscapes,
even the frozen scar of a frown
so like a familiar horizon.

*Jeremiad Johnson*                              *Tim Hawkins*

## About the Author

Tim Hawkins lives with his wife and three children in his hometown of Grand Rapids, Michigan, where he works in communications in the health care and biomedical research industry. In his younger days, he worked his way through high school, college and after at a host of jobs including dishwasher, busboy, fry cook, waiter, bartender, landscaper, house painter, door-to-door canvasser, telemarketer, taxi driver, soap factory line worker, Alaskan fish cannery slime-table worker, stevedore, nose-hair clipper model and Taiwan cram school teacher. After graduating from University of Michigan, he worked his way around the world for the better part of two decades, studying the Spanish and Chinese languages and working as a journalist, technical writer, grant writer, adjunct professor and teacher in international schools.

To date, he has published well over 100 works of short fiction, non-fiction and poetry in more than 40 print and online magazines, been nominated for the Pushcart Prize, Best of the Net and Best Microfiction, and served as preliminary judge for the 47th Annual Dyer-Ives Poetry Competition (2015) judged by Mark Doty. His poetry collection, **Wanderings at Deadline**, was published in 2012 by Aldrich Press. Find out more at his website: ***www.timhawkinspoetry.com***

www.ingramcontent.com/pod-product-compliance
Lightning Source LLC
Chambersburg PA
CBHW030458010526
44118CB00011B/996